THE TRANSFORMATIONAL ADVENTURE

STUDY GUIDE

BY ALAN & INDA WILLIAMS
WITH KERI WYATT KENT

ISBN 978-0-9909222-6-1
Printed in the United States of America

THE TRANSFORMATIONAL ADVENTURE

STUDY GUIDE

CONTENTS

WELCOME TO THE ADVENTURE

Something within us longs for adventure, yearns to be part of something bigger than ourselves. We have this feeling that life should offer more than what our ordinary days provide. Some will try to fulfill that longing by scaling mountains, running marathons, or climbing the career ladder.

Mountain climbing is exhilarating. Business success can be exciting. But our longing for adventure can never be met by engaging in extreme sports or amassing wealth—or just dreaming about those things. Why? Because we were made to live an adventure that happens only when we follow Jesus—when we take risks not for the adrenaline rush they offer, but because of the eternal consequences they impact. I have lived in both spaces, and the latter is so much more adventurous!

The life of faith is not for the faint of heart. We mistakenly believe it's tame, but faith is only boring when we keep it safe and convenient for ourselves and the people around us. In reality, faith is the ultimate adventure!

The study in your hands is a challenge to change. To find a path of faith, and discover the life that is truly life. A more abundant life! Whether you are just beginning your spiritual journey or you've been walking with God for years, this study is for you. It's an invitation to transformation, to a deeper, more meaningful, walk of faith.

In almost anything in life (sports, business, relationships) you get out of something what you're willing to put into it. Just show up for work and put in your time, and you probably won't experience accelerated career advancement. Go to the gym and do some mild exercise in between chats with friends, and you may not see much change in your fitness level. Give your spouse, kids, or friends the leftovers of your time and energy, and you probably won't find the love and support you need and want. In fact, you might even end up lonely.

But the opposite is true as well: go all in, and you'll get a lot out.

The same is true for this study. Over the next seven lessons, you're going to learn a lot—if you're willing to engage. Don't worry, you don't need to be an expert. In fact, it's better if you can humbly admit you're not one. Just bring enthusiasm and a willingness to learn, and ask God to teach you.

These studies correspond to the videos at http://www.TransformationalAdventure.com. They are also meant to supplement the books in the Transformational Adventure series, which are available on the website (and on Amazon) as well.

Here are some simple recommendations and a bit of an overview about what to expect in each lesson.

Before each study, read over the lesson to familiarize yourself with the Scriptures and the questions. You don't need to do "homework" and write out your answers before the meeting, because part of what you'll be discussing will be presented via video at the meeting. But knowing what to expect will give you time to reflect and pray prior to the meeting. If you like, you can look up the Bible passages in other translations to compare them. (You can find about 40 different English translations on www.biblegateway.com or similar sites.)

Each lesson consists of the following components:

OPEN: These open-ended questions may feel light or simple, but they provide an opportunity for everyone to "warm up" to the discussion and get comfortable. During this part of the meeting, focus on listening carefully to other group members in order to get to know them better. You don't have to have every person answer every question. Let everyone share (or not) at the level that feels comfortable to them.

WATCH: Here, you will watch the video for the session, which can be found at www.TransformationalAdventure.com.

NOTES: This page provides space for you to take notes on what you hear and see in the video. Jot down ideas that strike you or questions that come to mind as you watch. What key ideas do you want to remember? What questions come up as you watch and listen? Each video includes three revelations or key points. These are listed in the notes section with some keywords left out so you can fill in the blanks as you listen and see them on the screen. (If you need the full text of each revelation, you may find that in the appendix.) Refer to your notes as you discuss the video and Scriptures with your group.

READ: This section is simply a passage or two of Scripture related to the topic of the lesson. You'll have one person read it aloud, or you can ask several people to read, each reading just a few sentences. Feel free to underline words or phrases that stand out to you, or jot notes in the margins as you read together.

RESPOND: This section allows you to learn by talking it over—and by listening to the insights of other group members. This should make up the bulk of your meeting time. Allow plenty of time— we recommend at least 45 minutes—to discuss the questions. If your group is larger than 7 or 8, you might want to divide into two smaller groups for this part of the meeting, just to give everyone adequate time to share. Doing this will allow you to go deeper in your discussion of the teaching and storytelling, dig into the Scripture you just read, and explore and wrestle with how to live out what you're learning. Again, there's no pressure. **Every person does not need to answer every question**—whoever would like to speak may do so, but you always have the right to "pass" on a question. Share as much of your story as feels safe. (Early on, it would be a good idea to agree, out loud, to confidentiality—what is shared in the group, stays in the group.) Strive to make other group members feel comfortable by listening to them with empathy and compassion. Resist the urge to "fix" each other! Instead, receive each other with compassion, and respect each person's perspective.

DIVE DEEPER: This optional section is for those who would like to study more of what the Bible says about each lesson's topic, to dive a little deeper into God's word. Optimally, you'd take the time between meetings to work through this section a little at a time. This section is for individual study and journaling, not necessarily group discussion. Some groups choose to allot a few minutes at the beginning of each meeting for people to share what they've learned during individual study time.

RESOURCES: Here, you'll find some Bible commentary, footnotes and a deeper look at the Scriptures and their context. This section will help you understand and apply the Bible verses in the lesson.

ACTION STEP: These are suggested steps that you can take to learn more or live out what you've learned. These will challenge you not just to think about an adventure, but actually take steps to begin one. This is the most important part of transformation: putting what you learn into action.

SALVATION

THE WAKE UP CALL OF A LIFETIME

[1]

A wake-up call: that moment, that event, maybe an actual phone call, that changes everything. Most of us would say we've had at least one pivotal moment like that in our lives. The question is, does that call—that turning point, that decision—actually wake us up? Does it get our attention, turn us in a new direction? Or do we just keep on with business as usual?

Many of us are taught our whole lives to compete, to push through pain, to just try harder when things get difficult. But what if God wanted to speak to us through our pain? What if he wanted to use our challenges to bring us into closer relationship with himself? What if we responded to life's wake up calls by actually waking up, by responding to God's invitation to live with meaning and purpose beyond our own success?

(Romans 10:9-11, NIV)

If you declare with your mouth, "Jesus is Lord," and believe in your heart that God raised him from the dead, you will be saved. For it is with your heart that you believe and are justified, and it is with your mouth that you profess your faith and are saved. As Scripture says, "Anyone who believes in him will never be put to shame."

OPEN

◆ *Is there something you have seen in the news or an incident that happened to you or a friend, that has made you second-guess justice in America?*

_____

_____

_____

//

◆ *Tell about a time when you felt you were unfairly punished by a parent, teacher, or boss.*

_____

_____

_____

//

◆ *What happened? How did that feel?*

_____

_____

_____

WATCH VIDEO

WATCH THE VIDEO **FOR THIS SESSION NOW.**
VIDEO ACCESS: http://www.TransformationalAdventure.com/heart

SESSION NOTES

1. Acting _____ does not make you a _____ .

2. Thinking is not _____ .

3. Feeling _____ often means we're _____ .

_____
_____
_____
_____
_____
_____

READ

Ephesians 2:1-10, NASB //

And you were dead in your trespasses and sins, [2] in which you formerly walked according to the course of this world, according to the prince of the power of the air, of the spirit that is now working in the sons of disobedience. [3] Among them we too all formerly lived in the lusts of our flesh, indulging the desires of the flesh and of the mind, and were by nature children of wrath, even as the rest. [4] But God, being rich in mercy, because of His great love with which He loved us, [5] even when we were dead in our transgressions, made us alive together with Christ (by grace you have been saved), [6] and raised us up with Him, and seated us with Him in the heavenly places in Christ Jesus, [7] so that in the ages to come He might show the surpassing riches of His grace in kindness toward us in Christ Jesus. [8] For by grace you have been saved through faith; and that not of yourselves, it is the gift of God; [9] not as a result of works, so that no one may boast. [10] For we are His workmanship, created in Christ Jesus for good works, which God prepared beforehand so that we would walk in them.

Before I came to faith with Jesus in my heart, a friend and mentor of mine quoted Ephesians 2:8-9 to me numerous times, trying to help me really understand grace, but I didn't "get it." I acted as if I had received Jesus in my heart, but I really hadn't. I was going through the motions, fooling everyone including myself. Then, at age 43, I realized that I might understand them on a surface level in my mind, but did not understand them, not in my heart. And the depth of these verses are bottomless, unending, limitless....Ironically, when I finally understood them, I realized no one can ever fully understand the depth of these verses. –Alan Williams

RESPOND

◆ *Read carefully through the passage from Ephesians again. What does this text say God has done for us? Go through and underline things God has done for us. As a group, make a list of those things you find in this passage. Which of these do you find most surprising? Briefly explain.*

_____

_____

_____

◆ *What do you think it means to be "saved by grace through faith" (vs. 8-9)? Use the context around this verse to help you determine its meaning.*

_____

_____

_____

◆ In the video, you heard Alan describe himself as being "lukewarm" before he fully opened his heart to God, even though he went to church and read his Bible. What does a person with lukewarm faith look like? In what ways might they appear to be a Christian or at least a "good person"? What are that person's chances of going to heaven, do you think?

_____

_____

_____

◆ In the video, Alan talked about realizing that Satan is real. What does this passage say about Satan and his influence?

_____

_____

_____

◆ What is the difference between thinking something is true "with your head," and believing in someone completely with your heart?

_____

_____

_____

◆ Alan's heart surgery was a "wake-up call" to live and believe differently. Tell about a time you experienced a "wake-up call" in life. What happened? Identify one specific thing you changed as a result.

_____

_____

_____

DIVE DEEPER

(This section is for personal study between meetings.)

"But now the righteousness of God apart from the law is revealed, being witnessed by the Law and the Prophets, even the righteousness of God, through faith in Jesus Christ, to all and on all who believe. For there is no difference; for all have sinned and fall short of the glory of God, being justified freely by His grace through the redemption that is in Christ Jesus..."

Romans 3:21-24
NKJV

◆ When we have faith to believe in Jesus, what does this passage tell us that God gives us?

_____

_____

_____

◆ What does it mean to "fall short of the glory of God"? According to Romans 3, who falls short? What do you think it means to be "justified freely"? How can we be justified in God's eyes?

_____

_____

_____

"For God so loved the world that He gave His only begotten Son, that whoever believes in Him should not perish but have everlasting life."

John 3:16
NKJV

◆ *What motivates God, according to this verse?*

_____

_____

_____

◆ *What promise do you find in this verse?*

_____

_____

_____

◆ *How would you describe the difference between thinking that Jesus is the way to eternal life, and actually believing in Jesus? Which of these most accurately describes your current relationship with Jesus?*

_____

_____

_____

Say the welcoming word to God—"Jesus is my Master"—embracing, body and soul, God's work of doing in us what he did in raising Jesus from the dead. That's it. You're not "doing" anything; you're simply calling out to God, trusting him to do it for you. That's salvation. With your whole being you embrace God setting things right, and then you say it, right out loud: "God has set everything right between him and me!"

Romans 10:9–10

The Message

◆ *What does it mean to embrace God with your whole being?*

_____

_____

_____

◆ *What is the difference between thinking God is real and saying "Jesus is my Master"? How would declaring Jesus as your Master change your current attitudes and actions?*

_____

_____

_____

◆ *What do you think it means to "call out to God, trusting him to do it for you"?*

_____

_____

_____

THE WALKING DEAD
Ephesians 2:1, 5

Paul writes about "being dead" in our sins, even though we're alive physically. While it might seem like metaphorical language, Paul is pointing toward an important truth about us: we are not just physical beings, but spiritual ones as well, and without Jesus, we are spiritually dead.

We can seem very alive; we can even go through the motions of acting like a religious person—to the point where we even fool ourselves! But what brings us to life, spiritually, is not our own efforts at good behavior, but trusting Christ alone with our whole lives.

RESOURCES

THE PRINCE OF THE POWER OF THE AIR
Ephesians 2:2

Again, Paul writes about a spiritual reality: Satan is real. He influences us, whispers lies, tries to confuse us. Satan does not necessarily want us to go out and do awful things. He'd rather confuse and deceive us and make us think we have a pretty good chance of getting into heaven, because we're pretty good. He'd rather deceive us into thinking our religious words and pious actions will make us right with God, He would have us embrace complacency, as we practice a comfortable and convenient religion. The truth is, that lie keeps us from really knowing God—which is exactly what Satan wants. Where do you see the "ruler of the air" attempting to exert influence and authority in your life?

BELIEVE IN HIM
John 3:16

In our culture and language, we tend to understand "thinking" and "believing" are the same. We use the word believe as a general attitude, thought, and even wishful thinking. It is commonly misunderstood. For example:

- *I believe I will get a good job.*
- *I believe I will be rich.*
- *I believe I will win a championship.*
- *I believe I will go to heaven.*
- *I believe that Jesus Christ is the Son of God, who died for my sins and rose from the dead.*

As an English-speaking nation, we can easily swap out the word believe with think in the sentences above. I think I will be rich. I think I will win a championship. And yes...I think I will go to heaven.

The word in our Bible translated "believe" is the Greek word pisteuo which means an "absolute belief or confidence in certain divine truths." It goes far beyond just thinking something is true. An absolute is something you have a surety about. You know it will come to be, like a warranty or guarantee.

John 3:16 does not say, "whoever believes Him" (in other words, believes what He says is the truth). Rather, it says, "whoever believes IN Him." True, saving faith requires us to trust in Jesus, not in ourselves. Belief goes beyond intellectual understanding of Jesus, to an intimate relationship with Jesus. A relationship that is more certain than the ones you have with your spouse, children, relatives, or friends. A relationship where you know that you know that you know . . . and He knows you!

ACTION STEPS

The passage we studied reminds us that "God is rich in mercy." Between now and the next session, during your time with God, list some specific ways in which God has shown you mercy.

Then, try this experiment: each day, choose to show mercy to someone you interact with. It might be a co-worker, your spouse, your kids, or a random stranger (maybe the guy who cuts you off in traffic). Instead of revenge or competition or even giving someone what they deserve, choose mercy. Make this a daily habit—live a life of mercy that reflects God's mercy to you.

Report back to the group on how this goes. What happens? How does this experiment impact your relationship with God? With other people?

SESSION NOTES

BROKENNESS

A DEATH SENTENCE THAT BROUGHT LIFE

[2]

(Philippians 4:6-7, NKJV)

Be anxious for nothing, but in everything by prayer and supplication, with thanksgiving, let your requests be made known to God; and the peace of God, which surpasses all understanding, will guard your hearts and minds through Christ Jesus.

Our culture values and rewards self-sufficiency. We admire the "self-made man" and measure success with a financial yardstick. And yet, these traits work against us and keep us from experiencing the Holy Spirit. Our self-sufficiency keeps us living in the flesh, rather than living by the Spirit. Though chasing financial success to the exclusion of spiritual endeavors might make us comfortable, it will never allow us to really experience the Comforter, the Counselor, the Holy Spirit.

What does it mean to live by the Spirit? That's what we're going to talk about in this session. Sometimes, we discover this relationship when we go through painful or difficult circumstances. The good news is, God is always right there with us. He's a good Father, which sometimes means he allows us to experience the consequences of our actions. He's not capricious or punitive, but never promises our life with be painless either.

In this fallen world, bad things happen sometimes. The Bible tells us Satan roams like a hungry lion, seeking to devour. In fact, we live each day in a battle with Satan. Thinking and believing "God gave me this problem" can keep us from engaging in important spiritual battles that will ultimately strengthen our faith (see sidebar). When the evil one sends trials our way, God comforts, guides and helps us. As a result, we grow closer to Him and deeper in our faith.

"The way you think about life's struggles matters greatly. When I assumed that life's trials were given to me by God, I didn't fight them. After all, why should I resist God and his perfect plan? Even if that plan seemed imperfect to me, he must be giving me struggles for a reason, right? But that kind of thinking kept me from engaging in the spiritual battle Satan was waging against me, which enabled him to prevail against me. When I began to identify Satan as the source of my life's challenges, everything changed. I was able to fully engage in the battle, call on the spiritual weapons God provided, and experience victory."

—Alan Williams

OPEN

◆ *What's one idea or concept from the previous session that stuck with you since we last gathered?*

_____

_____

_____

//

◆ *Read the opening Scripture from this lesson from Philippians, which promises "peace that surpasses all understanding." Tell about a time you experienced peace that surpassed understanding, perhaps in the midst of struggle or trial. What happened? How did your attitudes or actions change as a result?*

_____

_____

_____

_____

_____

_____

WATCH VIDEO

WATCH THE VIDEO **FOR THIS SESSION NOW.**
VIDEO ACCESS: http://www.TransformationalAdventure.com/cancer

SESSION NOTES

1. *God can be* _____ .

2. *God's love gives us* _____ *and* _____.

3. *God* _____ *us through other* _____ .

_____

_____

_____

_____

_____

_____

READ

Romans 8:5-6, and 24-28, NKJV //

5 For those who live according to the flesh set their minds on the things of the flesh, but those who live according to the Spirit, the things of the Spirit. 6 For to be carnally minded is death, but to be spiritually minded is life and peace....

24 For we were saved in this hope, but hope that is seen is not hope; for why does one still hope for what he sees? 25 But if we hope for what we do not see, we eagerly wait for it with perseverance.

26 Likewise the Spirit also helps in our weaknesses. For we do not know what we should pray for as we ought, but the Spirit Himself makes intercession for us with groanings which cannot be uttered. 27 Now He who searches the hearts knows what the mind of the Spirit is, because He makes intercession for the saints according to the will of God.

28 And we know that all things work together for good to those who love God, to those who are the called according to His purpose.

"Many years separate the day I received Jesus as my Savior and the day I received Him as my Lord. In this world of self-sufficiency, many of us don't lack for much when you really consider what we already have. I fear that this state of contentment leads to complacency, to the point that many of us never find a need to surrender our will to Jesus. Until we receive that wake-up call. When we're faced with something that is so big and beyond our control (for us it was cancer), we are forced to look beyond ourselves for help. This is the silver lining. This is the blessing. This is the hope." —Inda Williams

RESPOND

◆ In the video, Alan talks about how Inda's faith and trust in God helped him get through the experience of cancer. Tell about a time someone else's faith helped you get through a time when your faith faltered.

_____

_____

_____

◆ In the video, Inda said that before Alan's cancer diagnosis, they "had lived self-sufficient lives." In what ways does your self-sufficiency keep God at arms' length?

_____

_____

_____

◆ What does it mean to set your mind on the things of the Spirit? What, specifically, would you think about?

_____

_____

_____

◆ *Look at the passage from Romans 8. What promises do you find in this text? Underline them and share them with the group. What specific things does the Holy Spirit do to help us when we are weak?*

_____

_____

_____

◆ *Romans 8:28 says that "all things work together for good to those who love God." If that's true, why do people get cancer or have other struggles? How did good come from Alan's cancer diagnosis? What is the difference between "good" and "easy"? Tell about a time when a difficult circumstance brought about some unexpected good in your life.*

_____

_____

_____

_____

DIVE DEEPER

(This section is for personal study between meetings.)

"Trust in the Lord with all your heart,
And lean not on your own understanding;
In all your ways acknowledge Him,
And He shall direct your paths."

Proverbs 3:5-6
NKJV

◆ *What does it mean to "lean on your own understanding"?*

_____

_____

◆ *What specific situation are you facing right now where you struggle to trust God? Spend some time praying about that situation right now and turn it over to God.*

_____

_____

◆ *Notice that the word "all" is repeated in the passage above. Why is this word important? Are you "all in" when it comes to trusting God and acknowledging him?*

_____

_____

"And not only that, but we also glory in tribulations, knowing that tribulation produces perseverance; 4 and perseverance, character; and character, hope. 5 Now hope does not disappoint, because the love of God has been poured out in our hearts by the Holy Spirit who was given to us."

Romans 5:3-5
NKJV

◆ *What do you think it means to "glory in tribulations"?*

_____

_____

◆ *What tribulations are you currently facing?*

_____

_____

◆ *According to this verse, life often follows this sequence:*
tribulation -->perseverance-->character-->hope.
Think about a time when you saw this sequence unfold in your own life. How did persevering through trials strengthen your character and ultimately give you hope?

_____

_____

◆ *How is our hope connected to the Holy Spirit?*

_____

_____

HOPE

When the Bible talks about hope, it is not just a vague wishful thinking, but a specific and eager expectation. The Greek word is elpis, meaning a joyful and confident anticipation.

RESOURCES

HOLY SPIRIT

The Holy Spirit is not just an aspect of God's nature or character; He is a person within the Trinity. The original language of the Bible refers to the Holy Spirit as the paraclete, which comes from the same root as English words like parallel or paralegal. The word is hard to translate precisely into English, and different translators have chosen words like Counselor, Comforter, Helper, Advocate—all of which point to the complexity and beauty of the Holy Spirit and what he does. He is the one who comes alongside us, who transforms us.

The Holy Spirit interacts with us in many ways:
- He heals us.
- He convicts us of sin.
- He empowers us with gifts.
- He advocates and intercedes for us.

See John 14:26 and John 16:6-8 for more on the power and influence of the Holy Spirit.

ACTION STEPS

Set aside about a half hour to be alone with God. Turn OFF your phone; step away from your computer. Sit somewhere where you will not be interrupted or distracted. Perhaps you'll want to go to a place where you can enjoy a view of nature, or to a room where you can have privacy.

Once you are in this place, take a few minutes to just sit quietly. Let go of any worries or thoughts about the rest of your day. Try to be fully present, not thinking about the past or the future. For now, don't even bring your prayer requests or needs. Your goal is to simply be with God, to experience the presence of the Holy Spirit.

God is always with us, present everywhere. We don't have to ask him to "be with us" because he always is—but most of the time we're oblivious. In this quiet moment, simply ask God to make you aware of his presence. Worship God for who he is. You may want to pray a simple prayer, such as "Lord, surround me with your love," or "Holy Spirit, fill me," or "Thank you for loving me."

Simply rest in God's presence. Pay attention, spiritually. Let yourself feel God's love wrap around you, as close as the air you breathe. Welcome the Holy Spirit, and allow him to touch your heart.

SESSION NOTES

(2 Corinthians 12:9 NKJV)

And He said to me, "My grace is sufficient for you, for My strength is made perfect in weakness." Therefore most gladly I will rather boast in my infirmities, that the power of Christ may rest upon me.

RESTORATION

PAIN THAT BROUGHT HEALING

[3]

God's grace is what saves us from sin and from an eternity separated from him. But if we see grace as something that is mere "fire insurance" to rescue us from God's judgment, we miss out on something profound: God's grace is available to us not just someday, but right now. We can receive miracles right now. We can be healed—physically, relationally, spiritually—not just in the life to come, but in this life, today. Grace brings restoration and healing.

To live in God's sufficient grace, we must get to the place where we stop relying on our own strength, our own smarts, our own accomplishments. Sometimes, difficulties or infirmities take us to a place where we can more fully experience grace. We discover that God's power truly is made perfect in our weakness. Even if we aren't going through a catastrophic illness, sooner or later we hit challenges that force us to realize our own limits. That can seem difficult at the time, but it's a spiritual opportunity. Abundant life happens when we learn that he can be trusted.

Like the manna God fed the Israelites, God gives us enough strength for one day at a time. He wants us to rely on him—not as a way of controlling us, but as a gift to us. God knows that when we rely on his daily grace to sustain us, we live in the most joyful, intimate place we can on this earth. It is the best way to live, the way to access the life that is truly life.

OPEN

◆ *In the last session, your "action step" was to spend time alone with God, focusing on the Holy Spirit. How did this go? (It's okay if it felt difficult or awkward.) What did you experience during this time with God?*

_____

_____

_____

///

◆ *When you were growing up, what messages did you receive about strength and weakness? How does our culture view weakness or dependence?*

_____

_____

_____

WATCH VIDEO

WATCH THE VIDEO **FOR THIS SESSION NOW.**
VIDEO ACCESS: *http://www.TransformationalAdventure.com/chemo*

SESSION NOTES

1. Facing _____ we can choose to _____ .

2. _____ in God builds our _____ in him.

3. _____ in God brings hope and _____ .

_____

_____

_____

_____

_____

_____

_____

READ

Ephesians 3:14-21, NKJV   //

¹⁴ For this reason I bow my knees to the Father of our Lord Jesus Christ, ¹⁵ from whom the whole family in heaven and earth is named, ¹⁶ that He would grant you, according to the riches of His glory, to be strengthened with might through His Spirit in the inner man, ¹⁷ that Christ may dwell in your hearts through faith; that you, being rooted and grounded in love, ¹⁸ may be able to comprehend with all the saints what is the width and length and depth and height— ¹⁹ to know the love of Christ which passes knowledge; that you may be filled with all the fullness of God.

²⁰ Now to Him who is able to do exceedingly abundantly above all that we ask or think, according to the power that works in us, ²¹ to Him be glory in the church by Christ Jesus to all generations, forever and ever. Amen.

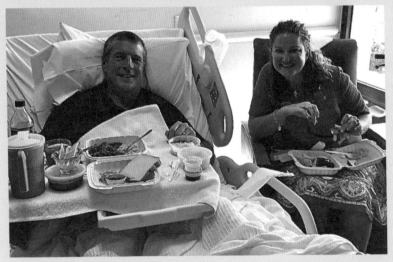

"As I began the chemo treatments, the outpouring of care and support showed me how much I was loved by people regardless of my performance. And this opened up my mind to trust the Spirit of God . . . or otherwise succumb to the negative side effects of the treatments. I began to receive our heavenly Father's love—something I didn't know existed. I didn't even know how much I needed His love. And this is where the healing began. I allowed Him to love me more and heal me as I learned to let Him love me. He healed me. I don't know which was first, but as I grew in my relationship with God, I was healed and restored in both spheres of health."

—Alan Williams, *Hidden Blessings from Chemo*

RESPOND

◆ In the video, Alan said that going through chemo forced him to rest and taught him to trust God. How are resting in God and trusting him related? In your life, what gets in the way of resting and trusting?

_____

_____

_____

◆ In the passage from Ephesians, we read that the writer (the Apostle Paul) prayed that his readers would "be strengthened with might through His Spirit in the inner man" (vs. 16). What do you think it means to be strengthened in the inner man (or woman)? According to the text, how does this strengthening happen?

_____

_____

_____

◆ *What does it mean to be "rooted and grounded in love" (vs. 17)? Alan described a daily practice of getting up early to pray and spend time with God that gave him strength to get through each day. Restoring himself spiritually restored and strengthened him physically. What do you do to stay "rooted and grounded in love"?*

_____

_____

_____

◆ *What keeps us from knowing "the width and length and depth and height" (vs. 18) of God's love? What happens to our strength and our faith when our view of God is too small?*

_____

_____

_____

◆ *In the video, Alan told about being healed and protected from the negative side effects of the Interferon chemotherapy. What is your response to his testimony? Where do you need healing—physically, emotionally, or spiritually—in your life? Based on Alan's testimony, what is your next step in trusting God for that healing?*

_____

_____

_____

_____

DIVE DEEPER

(This section is for personal study between meetings.)

Now the people complained about their hardships in the hearing of the Lord, and when he heard them his anger was aroused. Then fire from the Lord burned among them and consumed some of the outskirts of the camp. 2 When the people cried out to Moses, he prayed to the Lord and the fire died down. 3 So that place was called Taberah, because fire from the Lord had burned among them. 4 The rabble with them began to crave other food, and again the Israelites started wailing and said, "If only we had meat to eat! 5 We remember the fish we ate in Egypt at no cost—also the cucumbers, melons, leeks, onions and garlic. 6 But now we have lost our appetite; we never see anything but this manna!"

Numbers 11:1-6

NIV

◆ Why were the Israelites complaining?

_____

_____

◆ How did God respond to the Israelites' complaining? How do you think God
   responds to our complaining today?

_____

_____

_____

◆ In the video, Alan talks about how a friend challenged him to stop complaining,
   even though he was going through a very painful experience. He said, "If you don't
   quit complaining, you're never going to reach the Promised Land, the abundant
   life . . . that is on our doorstep if we just go out and get it, to receive it." In what
   circumstances are you most tempted to complain? What Promised Land are you
   trying to reach?

_____

_____

_____

◆ How does complaining get in the way of growth?

_____

_____

²² But the fruit of the Spirit is love, joy, peace, longsuffering, kindness, goodness, faithfulness, ²³ gentleness, self-control. Against such there is no law. ²⁴ And those who are Christ's have crucified the flesh with its passions and desires. ²⁵ If we live in the Spirit, let us also walk in the Spirit.

Galatians 5:22-25
NKJV

◆ *In the video, Alan said that because he was so driven, he often "missed the joy" God had for him. But being forced to rest restored his joy. Look at the attributes that make up the fruit of the Spirit, listed in verse 22 and 23. Which element(s) of the whole fruit is/are missing in your life? Which one do you most earnestly desire?*

_____

_____

◆ *What do you think it means to "walk in the Spirit" (vs. 25)?*

_____

_____

◆ *How might walking in the Spirit (and resting in His presence) bring about the fruit that God's given you a desire for?*

_____

_____

_____

EXCEEDINGLY ABUNDANTLY
Ephesians 3:20

We might mistakenly think that an "abundant life" has to do with material wealth, or the absence of problems in our life. As Alan and Inda's story shows, the abundant life is really about receiving God's presence and hope, even in the midst of difficult circumstances. God did not give Alan cancer but this incredibly sovereign God obviously allows us to go through difficulties. Even in the midst of those difficulties, he is always behind us, waiting for us to turn around and ask for his help. In fact, he healed Alan miraculously, and he used the struggle to show Alan his power. An abundant life is about experiencing grace that is more than sufficient, and if we have faith, it can mean we'll experience miracles. Abundant life is about restoring relationships with God and with others. God exceeds our expectations and is able to give us an abundance of love, joy, grace, and peace, in spite of our circumstances.

RESOURCES

"THE RABBLE WITH THEM"
Numbers 11:4

This phrase refers to the Egyptians who traveled with the Israelites. (Sometimes called the "mixed multitude." See Exodus 12:38.) Their cravings were greedy—they wanted not just sustenance but rich food. Their complaints then led to the Israelites "wailing." Obviously, the rabble's bad attitude was contagious! Not satisfied with manna, they wanted more. God responds by sending quail, in huge numbers. Their greed causes them to overeat and gag on the quail. The text tells us that even as they were eating the quail, God struck them with a plague (See Numbers 11:31-35.) to punish their greed. Could it be that after eating manna for a long time, then gorging themselves on rich meat, they got sick from the change in diet? While God does not capriciously send us difficulties, He does sometimes allow us to experience the consequence of our actions and our greed. It's as if God says, "You want meat? I'll give you meat! So much you'll get sick of it." (See Numbers 11:19-20.) As Alan's friend gently admonished him, complaining keeps us from experiencing the full blessings of God. When we learn to be satisfied with God's provision (daily manna), we realize that his grace is sufficient.

THE FRUIT OF THE SPIRIT
Galatians 5:22-23

This verse describes the fruit, or result, of the Spirit's influence on our lives. It is not a to-do list that we must achieve in order to earn God's love. Just the opposite—it describes what the Holy Spirit does to transform us. It describes the results of the work of the Spirit, not the results of our efforts. Nor is it a list of "fruit," but a description of various aspects of "the fruit," or result, of having the Spirit guide our lives. This kind of fruit grows in our lives not by our working extra hard to be loving or patient, but rather, when we align ourselves with God, abide in Christ, and allow the Spirit to guide us.

This passage makes an excellent tool for self-examination. Read through the passage and ask God to show you ways in which you are bearing fruit, and ways in which you are not. Again, this is not a to-do list, but a gentle way to see which particular areas of your life you might need to open up to the Spirit in deeper ways, allowing him to work and bring about real transformation. It can also help you see the ways in which the Holy Spirit has transformed you already—made you more loving, more patient, more kind, perhaps, than you were previously. Thank God for the work he's done, and trust him for the ways in which he will continue to work in your heart.

ACTION STEPS

Pay attention to your attitude. How often do you complain, even about small things (the traffic, your kids, your job)? Make every effort to notice your own complaining (even if it's just in your thoughts), and stop it. Try this experiment: fast from complaining. **Give it up, for one week, as a spiritual practice.** Enlist the help of a close friend or your spouse. Ask them to hold you accountable. Ask God to help you as well. Become aware of how complaining can sneak into your everyday conversations or thoughts. When you notice it, choose to simply stop. Replace the negative thought with a positive one. Instead of complaining, thank God for something. Choose to ask God for strength and perseverance in those moments. Notice what happens when you stop complaining. How does it affect your physical, emotional, and spiritual health? Use the notes page in this chapter to journal about this experience and your progress.

SESSION NOTES

POWER

[4]

(Galatians 6:2, 9-10, NKJV)

Bear one another's burdens, and so fulfill the law of Christ...And let us not grow weary while doing good, for in due season we shall reap if we do not lose heart. Therefore, as we have opportunity, let us do good to all, especially to those who are of the household of faith.

When we go through difficult circumstances, we tend to lean on the people around us. Though we need their help, we're not always gracious about it.

If you're the one being leaned upon, it can be exhausting. We might very well "become weary while doing good." Whether you're caring for a spouse who is ill, supporting someone who has lost a job or suffers from depression, or tending to the needs of a child or an aging parent, being a caregiver is not an easy job. However, when you lean on God, he can use you to bring about miracles, healing, and restoration.

We are called to love and support our brothers and sisters in Christ. In certain seasons of life, that caregiver role comes to the forefront. However, we can't sustain this in our own strength. Caregiving is an opportunity to lean on God and draw strength from him that far surpasses what we could do on our own. It's an opportunity for God to show his power and might—to surprise us with the strength he imparts to us. In this lesson, we'll focus on caregiving and how that role can offer us the opportunity to draw closer to God and receive his supernatural strength.

OPEN

♦ *In the previous lesson, your "action step" was to fast from complaining. How did that go? What challenges did you encounter as you attempted to stop complaining? What surprised you about this practice?*

_____

_____

_____

//

♦ *In this lesson we examine the importance of leaning on God when you are in a caregiver role. Tell about a season of your life when you had to be a caregiver (to a child, spouse, parent, friend, or relative). What challenges come with this role?*

_____

_____

_____

_____

_____

_____

WATCH VIDEO

WATCH THE VIDEO **FOR THIS SESSION NOW.**
VIDEO ACCESS: http://www.TransformationalAdventure.com/caregiver

SESSION NOTES

1. _____ continuously and confidently.

2. _____ boldy and _____ .

3. Clarify your _____ .

_____

_____

_____

_____

_____

_____

READ

James 5:13-16, NLT //

[13] Are any of you suffering hardships? You should pray. Are any of you happy? You should sing praises. [14] Are any of you sick? You should call for the elders of the church to come and pray over you, anointing you with oil in the name of the Lord. [15] Such a prayer offered in faith will heal the sick, and the Lord will make you well. And if you have committed any sins, you will be forgiven.

[16] Confess your sins to each other and pray for each other so that you may be healed. The earnest prayer of a righteous person has great power and produces wonderful results.

RESPOND

◆ *According to this passage in James, what is the relationship between prayer, faith, confession, and healing? Find those words in the passage, and explain how they are connected.*

_____

_____

◆ *This passage talks about not just praying for yourself, but having others pray for you. Why do you think God instructs us to pray in community?*

_____

_____

◆ *In the video, Inda said, "Words can bring life or death. Create an environment with your words. Choose your words wisely. . . . Positive words bring more peace and more spiritual alignment." Tell about a time that someone else's positive words brought you peace. Identify someone in your life right now who needs positive words and the spiritual alignment they provide. How can you help?*

_____

_____

_____

◆ Inda's gift of faith comforted Alan and ushered in miraculous healing. She was a conduit of God's power, and God enabled her to be strong during Alan's illness. What is your response to the idea of healing?

_____

_____

_____

◆ In the video, Inda shared this advice: "If you get disconnected from God, you're going to lose your source of strength, so rely heavily upon him." Tell about a time that you had to rely heavily upon God. How did he help you and give you strength?

_____

_____

_____

_____

DIVE DEEPER

(This section is for personal study between meetings.)

Jesus called his twelve disciples to him and gave them authority to drive out impure spirits and to heal every disease and sickness. [5] These twelve Jesus sent out with the following instructions: "Do not go among the Gentiles or enter any town of the Samaritans. [6] Go rather to the lost sheep of Israel. [7] As you go, proclaim this message: 'The kingdom of heaven has come near.' [8] Heal the sick, raise the dead, cleanse those who have leprosy, drive out demons. Freely you have received; freely give."

Matthew 10:1, 5-8
NIV

 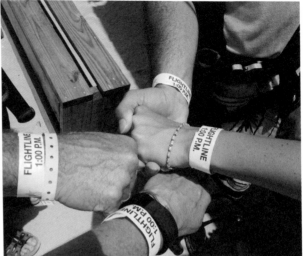

◆ Jesus told his disciples to proclaim that the kingdom of heaven has come near. What do you think that means?

_____

_____

◆ In the video, Inda said that Jesus has given all of us the authority to heal. This passage talks about that authority. What is your response to this idea? Have you ever used this authority?

_____

_____

◆ What had the disciples "freely received" from Jesus? What have you received from Jesus that you sense he is inviting you to "freely give" to others?

_____

_____

I look up to the mountains; does my strength come from mountains? No, my strength comes from God, who made heaven, and earth, and mountains. 3-4 He won't let you stumble, your Guardian God won't fall asleep. Not on your life! Israel's Guardian will never doze or sleep. 5-6 God's your Guardian, right at your side to protect you— Shielding you from sunstroke, sheltering you from moonstroke. 7-8 God guards you from every evil, he guards your very life. He guards you when you leave and when you return, he guards you now, he guards you always.

Psalm 121
THE MESSAGE

◆ *Read the Psalm aloud. Which verse or phrase stands out to you? It asks, rhetorically, if our strength comes from mountains. In our culture, what things (other than God) are people tempted to look to for strength?*

_____

_____

◆ *What promises from God do you find in this Scripture?*

_____

_____

◆ *In the Psalm we read that our strength comes from God. How do we access that strength? What do you think it means that God "guards" us?*

_____

_____

[7] Then Jesus said to them again, "Most assuredly, I say to you, I am the door of the sheep. [8] All who ever came before Me are thieves and robbers, but the sheep did not hear them. [9] I am the door. If anyone enters by Me, he will be saved, and will go in and out and find pasture. [10] The thief does not come except to steal, and to kill, and to destroy. I have come that they may have life, and that they may have it more abundantly. [11] I am the good shepherd. The good shepherd gives His life for the sheep."

John 10:7–11

NKJV

◆ *In verses 8 and 10, Jesus mentions "thieves and robbers." Who is he talking about? What does the thief do? What does Jesus, the Good Shepherd, do?*

_____

_____

◆ *What do you think Jesus means when he compares himself to a door (or in some Bible translations, a gate)?*

_____

_____

◆ *What promise do you find in verse 10? What is your response to this promise?*

_____

_____

_____

_____

THE LORD WILL MAKE YOU WELL
(JAMES 5:15)

Many of us assume, or are directly taught, that miraculous healings happened back in "biblical times" but don't happen today. And yet, many people (including Alan) experience miraculous healing today. God wants us to be well, and he can heal people today through a prayer of faith. While we cannot guarantee healing, it does happen, and our words, prayers, faith, and belief can bring God's power to bear on any situation—even cancer. Alan was healed of many side effects from what is normally a devastating chemotherapy. His leg, today, has no lymph nodes, because they were surgically removed. Yet his leg no longer swells or has pain, and functions normally, as if it had lymph nodes. The promise of healing through prayer was not just for long ago; it is a promise for today.

RESOURCES

GOD'S YOUR GUARDIAN
(PSALM 121)

If we stay close to him, God protects, guards, and guides us. Imagine that you are a celebrity or CEO and have a personal bodyguard—someone to protect you and watch out for you. Imagine that instead of staying with your bodyguard, you run away. You end up getting hurt. Is it the bodyguard's fault? Not really. If you leave the guard and go off on your own, you lose his protection. God helps, protects, and guards our life—if we stay close to him. But in some ways, that choice is up to us. We cannot wander far from God and then complain that he hasn't helped us. Lean on God, keep your heart aligned with him, and the Bible promises that he will guard us and be near to us.

THE KINGDOM OF HEAVEN
(MATTHEW 10:6)

Jesus taught more about the kingdom of heaven than any other topic. He compares it to a pearl of great price, a treasure, a mustard seed, a bit of yeast, and a fishing net (Matthew 13). He says he's given us the keys to this kingdom (Matthew 16:19), but that to enter it, we must become like little children (Matthew 18). He promises the kingdom to the poor in spirit and the persecuted (Matthew 5). The kingdom of heaven is not just a future reality, but something that is available to us here and now. It is a spiritual reality that impacts our daily lives, if we have eyes to see it.

ACTION STEPS

No matter what we are going through, we can often find someone who has struggles more challenging than our own. Yes, our own struggles are real, but even as we face them we can also be aware of the pain and problems of others. Between now and the next time the group meets, send a note or email of encouragement to someone you know is going through a struggle. Maybe someone you know is facing cancer, as Alan did, or unemployment, divorce, or loss of some kind. Reach out to that person and let them know that you are praying for them. (And don't just say you're praying—really do it!) If the person is open to it, go pray with them in person, and pray with faith for their healing and restoration. Speak encouraging words to them, reminding them of the hope and victory they have in Jesus.

SESSION NOTES

FORGIVENESS

LOVE THAT CHANGES EVERYTHING

[5]

> And be kind to one another, tenderhearted, forgiving one another, even as God in Christ forgave you.
>
> (Ephesians 4:32, NKJV)

Our earthly parents have an incredible influence on us—for better or worse. When a friend hurts our feelings, we might feel anger, sadness, or disappointment, but the pain is not nearly as deep as we feel when we're let down or criticized by our father or mother. Those wounds can run deep.

Because parents are human, they're going to make mistakes. Because we're human, we are going to wound our parents as well. But healing those wounds is possible when we do the hard work of forgiving one another.

Author Lew Smedes writes that forgiveness is not letting the other person off the hook, but rather, letting yourself off the hook. Author Andy Andrews teaches that forgiveness is not something we grant to another, but is something we give to ourselves. By forgiving those who hurt us, we free ourselves from being hurt over and over again as we remember and dwell on the offense. Freedom comes when we can forgive others as Christ forgave us. Letting the hurt go sets us free.

OPEN

◆ *The action step in the previous lesson was to reach out to someone who is hurting and encourage them. How did that go?*
What happened as a result?

_____

_____

_____

//

◆ *This session's topic is forgiveness. Why is it hard for people to forgive someone who has wronged them? What gets in the way of forgiveness?*

_____

_____

_____

WATCH VIDEO

WATCH THE VIDEO **FOR THIS SESSION NOW.**
VIDEO ACCESS: http://www.TransformationalAdventure.com/forgiveness

SESSION NOTES

1.   *God's love is* _____ .

2.   *God's love* _____ *our character and* _____ .

2.   *God's* _____ *enables* _____ .

_____

_____

_____

_____

_____

_____

_____

READ

Mark 11:25-26, NKJV   //

[25] "And whenever you stand praying, if you have anything against anyone, forgive him, that your Father in heaven may also forgive you your trespasses. [26] But if you do not forgive, neither will your Father in heaven forgive your trespasses."

"God is the original, master forgiver. Each time we grope our reluctant way through the minor miracle of forgiving, we are imitating his style. I am not at all sure that any of us would have had the imagination enough to see the possibilities in this way to heal the wrongs of this life had he not done it first."

—Lew Smedes, in The Art of Forgiving.

RESPOND

◆ In the video, Tyler described Alan as a father who gave "performance-based love" and was "a tough guy." At the time, Tyler felt like he had to earn his father's love by his achievements on the football field or in academics. How did this impact the relationship between father and son?

_____

_____

◆ How might having a father who loves "conditionally" impact a child's relationship with their heavenly Father, who loves unconditionally? As earthly parents, we are called to love our children (as best we can) in the way God loves. While we may fall short of that ideal, how does "conditional" love impact our children's view of God?

_____

_____

◆ *What does Jesus say we must do in order to receive God's forgiveness? (See Mark 11:26, also recorded in Matthew 6:15.) What is your response to Jesus' statement?*

_____

_____

◆ *Tyler describes a change he saw in Alan—from being a "tough guy" to seeing him exhibit the fruit of the Spirit. (See Galatians 5:22-23, which we studied in Session 3). He even said that now his father is like a different person than he was before. What caused this change in Alan? How did it impact the relationship with his son?*

_____

_____

◆ *In the video, Tyler said, "Forgiveness isn't something that you decide to do one day and then the next day, it's easy. Forgiveness is something you decide to do one day, and then the next it is harder than it was before. And then the next day it slowly gets easier. You have to go through a period of time where what was once swept under the rug is no longer swept under the rug." Tell about a time when you experienced what Tyler describes. In your situation, what got "swept under the rug"? What happened when you no longer kept it hidden or unspoken?*

_____

_____

◆ *Think about how God forgives you. Are there times when—despite his forgiveness— you continued to sin? Think of this from God's perspective. How might he feel about it? How does knowing that God forgives you even when you sin impact your ability to forgive others?*

_____

_____

DIVE DEEPER

(This section is for personal study between meetings.)

29 Watch the way you talk. Let nothing foul or dirty come out of your mouth. Say only what helps, each word a gift. 30 Don't grieve God. Don't break his heart. His Holy Spirit, moving and breathing in you, is the most intimate part of your life, making you fit for himself. Don't take such a gift for granted. 31-32 Make a clean break with all cutting, backbiting, profane talk. Be gentle with one another, sensitive. Forgive one another as quickly and thoroughly as God in Christ forgave you.

Eph. 4:29-32
The Message

◆ Our words have tremendous power. How can our words "break God's heart"?

_____

_____

◆ How do the words we say impact our relationship with God? Our relationship with others?

_____

_____

◆ What would happen if you said only words that help, making "each word a gift" to God and the people around you?

_____

_____

◆ How does this passage describe the Holy Spirit? Is this an accurate description of the Holy Spirit in your life?

_____

_____

◆ What situations or friends tempt you to engage in backbiting or profanity? What do you need to do to "make a clean break" from those situations or people?

_____

_____

¹² Therefore, as the elect of God, holy and beloved,
put on tender mercies, kindness, humility, meekness,
longsuffering; ¹³ bearing with one another, and forgiving
one another, if anyone has a complaint against another;
even as Christ forgave you, so you also must do.

Colossians 3:12–13
NKJV

◆ *What does verse 12 tell us about our identity? How does it describe us?*

_____

_____

◆ *How does that identity help us to obey this verse?*

_____

_____

◆ *How can you "put on" mercy, kindness, etc.?*

_____

_____

◆ *How does being forgiven help us to forgive others?*

_____

_____

FORGIVENESS

The Bible is clear about forgiveness: if we want God to forgive us, we must forgive others. There is an expected reciprocity: you've been forgiven, so you should forgive. And if you don't forgive, you won't be forgiven. This task might seem impossible, because it often is impossible—in our own human weakness. God tells us to forgive, but he also enables us to forgive in ways we could not do without his help.

Forgiveness does not depend on the other person apologizing. While it's always wonderful to get an apology, we can decide to forgive—and free ourselves from the burden of resentment and pain—regardless of whether the person who wronged us ever apologizes.

Forgiveness is not the same thing as reconciliation. For example, suppose a woman is married to a man who physically abuses her.

In order to be safe—and to keep their children safe—that wife might need to move out to a safe space. Eventually, with help from a therapist and wise counsel, she might choose to forgive her abuser. That would be one important step. A separate and different step would be to reconcile. However, forgiveness does not require reconciliation. They both can happen, but they are not inextricable from one another. She could forgive him but not necessarily reconcile with him, as if nothing had happened, especially if he were unrepentant or didn't change his behavior. Sometimes, both forgiveness and reconciliation happen, but they are not the same thing. Forgiveness does not require the other person to apologize or repent, but reconciliation does. Clarity about this helps us to forgive.

RESOURCES

DON'T BREAK GOD'S HEART
Ephesians 4:30

Can we break God's heart? Does He feel sadness when he sees us being rebellious or refusing to forgive others? While we may not often consider God's feelings, he does have them. Just as a child's actions can impact a parent's feelings, so our actions and attitudes can either grieve or please God. Why? Because he loves us. He's invested in us; he cares about us and what we do. He wants the best for us, and he feels sad when we choose to sin or choose not to forgive. How we treat others impacts our relationship with God. We can't say we love God but hate—or refuse to forgive— other people. See also 1 John 2:8-11.

ACTION STEPS

Whom do you need to forgive? What would be the first step in that process? Perhaps it is writing a letter describing the exact nature of how that person wronged you. Even if you don't send the letter, writing down your thoughts and feelings can help you clarify what happened and why it hurt. Honestly own whatever part you played in the breakdown of this relationship, and express remorse and repentance. But also be clear about the ways in which the other person hurt you, how it made you feel. Then, write down your forgiveness of those wrongs. Let them go. Ask God to help you forgive, because he has forgiven you. It may be appropriate for you to burn this letter as a symbol of forgiving and letting go. Or, if you pray about it and feel you should share it with the person you're forgiving, you might want to have a face-to-face meeting in which you read the letter to them. They can hear your tone of voice, see your eyes and expression, and better understand your desire to forgive and extend grace.

SESSION NOTES

GRACE

THE POWER TO TURN IT ALL AROUND

[6]

(Ephesians 2:4-5, NIV)

But because of his great love for us, God, who is rich in mercy, made us alive with Christ even when we were dead in transgressions—it is by grace you have been saved.

Life is hard. Sometimes, bad things happen—like cancer, the loss of a loved one, a financial setback. And yet, as we walk through those challenging times, we have an opportunity to learn to trust God. We have an opportunity to depend on him, and in so doing, experience love and grace in a way that we would not if everything were going just fine.

Our growth impacts the people around us. As we trust God more, as we experience more of his love, we're able to give that love to others. The reverse is also true. If we're harsh or legalistic, if we struggle to extend grace to others, it's often because we don't fully know and experience the love God has for us. When we see God as demanding or punitive, we will be demanding of others. We can't give away what we do not have.

Trials often come with a hidden gift: they allow us the uncomfortable privilege of having to lean on God, let go of self-sufficiency, and be filled with God's love. When that happens, we become better able to love the people around us—and be more open to receiving God's love through them.

OPEN

◆ *The previous lesson's action step asked you to work on forgiving someone. How did that go? Tell the group about one step you took toward forgiveness.*

_____

_____

_____

//

◆ *It's been said that justice is getting what you deserve, mercy is not getting what you deserve, and grace is getting what you don't deserve (for example, getting love when we deserve punishment). What's so amazing about grace?*

_____

_____

_____

_____

_____

WATCH VIDEO

WATCH THE VIDEO **FOR THIS SESSION NOW.**
VIDEO ACCESS: http://www.TransformationalAdventure.com/grace

SESSION NOTES

1. _____ *readies us for* _____ .

2. _____ *brings eternal perspective.*

3. *Receiving God's* _____ *allows us to* _____ _____ .

_____

_____

_____

_____

_____

_____

READ

James 1:2-4, 12, NIV //

2 Consider it pure joy, my brothers and sisters, whenever you face trials of many kinds, 3 because you know that the testing of your faith produces perseverance. 4 Let perseverance finish its work so that you may be mature and complete, not lacking anything.... 12 Blessed is the one who perseveres under trial because, having stood the test, that person will receive the crown of life that the Lord has promised to those who love him.

FULLER'S

"Because of his grace, I am at a completely different position than where I would be. . . . . Since cancer, since my dad had the change that he's had in his heart, instead of a passive father, he's been an intentional father, and that is a major difference in the role that he plays. God turned this potentially awful thing into a beautiful [thing]. . . . It was the best thing that could have happened to us. I still think that it was the best thing that happened in my life, as far as spiritual growth. It was just amazing to watch what God could do with brokenness, the beauty He could make from that."

—Dustin Williams

RESPOND

◆ According to this passage in James, how should we respond to trials in our lives (vs. 2)?

_____

_____

_____

◆ What promises do you find in this passage?

_____

_____

_____

◆ What does the testing of your faith produce (vs. 3-4)?

_____

_____

_____

◆ In the video, Dustin said that the season of his father's chemo treatment and his brother's two broken feet was "a horribly awesome time, because of the bonding, the dependency. We'd never been that close." Have you ever been through a time that was "horribly awesome"—a time where you went through struggles and trials, but saw growth and experienced grace as a result? Explain.

_____

_____

_____

◆ Imagine yourself in Alan's situation: you're struggling through chemo, and your son brings home bad grades, says college is "overrated" and then tells you his girlfriend is pregnant. How would you respond? What enabled Alan to respond the way he did? How did it impact his relationship with his son?

_____

_____

_____

DIVE DEEPER

(This section is for personal study between meetings.)

"I beseech you therefore, brethren, by the mercies of God, that you present your bodies a living sacrifice, holy, acceptable to God, which is your reasonable service. 2 And do not be conformed to this world, but be transformed by the renewing of your mind, that you may prove what is that good and acceptable and perfect will of God. "

Romans 12:1-2
NKJV

◆ A "living sacrifice" would seem like a contradiction: a sacrifice offered on an altar would not be alive. What do you think it means to be a living sacrifice?

_____

_____

◆ In what ways are you tempted to "be conformed to this world"? How do the ways of our world differ from the way of God's grace?

_____

_____

◆ According to this verse, how can we be transformed (i.e. changed)? What specifically would that look like in your life—what would change and how would that change occur?

_____

_____

²⁰ "I am praying not only for these disciples but also for all who will ever believe in me through their message. ²¹ I pray that they will all be one, just as you and I are one—as you are in me, Father, and I am in you. And may they be in us so that the world will believe you sent me. ²² "I have given them the glory you gave me, so they may be one as we are one.²³ I am in them and you are in me. May they experience such perfect unity that the world will know that you sent me and that you love them as much as you love me.²⁴ Father, I want these whom you have given me to be with me where I am. Then they can see all the glory you gave me because you loved me even before the world began!

John 17:20-24 (NLT)

◆ *What did Jesus ask for his followers?*

_____

_____

◆ *What does it mean to have oneness with God?*

_____

_____

◆ *What gets in the way of unity with other believers?*

_____

_____

◆ *How does our ability to extend grace to others impact our unity with them?*

_____

_____

◆ *In this passage, Jesus prays for "perfect unity." In the previous passage from Romans 12, we read about God's "perfect will." How are these two ideas related? How might our transformation lead to unity with others?*

_____

_____

¹⁷ Therefore, if anyone is in Christ, he is a new creation; old things have passed away; behold, all things have become new. ¹⁸ Now all things are of God, who has reconciled us to Himself through Jesus Christ, and has given us the ministry of reconciliation, ¹⁹ that is, that God was in Christ reconciling the world to Himself, not imputing their trespasses to them, and has committed to us the word of reconciliation. ²⁰ Now then, we are ambassadors for Christ, as though God were pleading through us: we implore you on Christ's behalf, be reconciled to God. ²¹ For He made Him who knew no sin to be sin for us, that we might become the righteousness of God in Him.

2 Corinthians 5:17-21 (NKJV)

◆ *What do you think it means to be "in Christ"?*

_____

_____

◆ *What happens as a result of us being "in Christ"?*

_____

_____

◆ *What do you think the "ministry of reconciliation" means? What particular situation are you currently facing where God might be inviting you to engage in the ministry of reconciliation?*

_____

_____

◆ *This passage says we are "ambassadors for Christ." What do ambassadors do? What, specifically, should we do as ambassadors for Christ? Spend some time praying, not just speaking to God but also listening to Him. Ask Him to show you where you can be a reconciler, where you can be an ambassador.*

_____

_____

PERSEVERANCE
(JAMES 1)

In our culture, where we want everything to happen instantly, perseverance is rare. We don't have a lot of opportunity to build this character quality. We get impatient just waiting for the microwave to finish. In the original language, the Greek word translated perseverance is hupomone, which means endurance, constancy, and patience. We build endurance by facing challenges—much as an athlete builds endurance by running longer, lifting more weight, challenging themselves physically. Perseverance is not passive, as in simply waiting something out. It is active patience that pushes through difficulties and refuses to despair, even when life is hard or the way forward seems to be full of roadblocks or impossible odds.

RESOURCES

AMBASSADOR
(2 CORINTHIANS 5)

An ambassador is a diplomat sent out to represent his own country in another country. His mission is peaceful protection of his own country's interests. He is not waging war, but, in many ways, waging peace. To be Christ's ambassador means to be an agent of understanding and peace, a person whose job it is to improve relations between Christ and those who don't know him. Do our interactions with those outside of the family of God help them to understand God and be reconciled to Him?

When we trust Christ, all things become new. And yet, we know by experience that we still struggle with sin, even after we've genuinely given our life to Jesus. Our old self might seem to be hanging on, rather than "passing away."

Transformation takes time. This process, sometimes called sanctification, doesn't happen overnight. God doesn't snap his fingers and make us completely different. And yet, we are changed—and we have the opportunity to learn and grow, to align our will with God's, to become new people. God invites us into a process, and we must respond with obedience. The more we lean in and follow him, the more we accept the invitation to let go of our old life and habits and imitate Jesus, the more we will change.

ACTION STEPS

In the video, we heard Dustin describe how he and his mother took care of his dad and brother. That caregiving role can be tiring and thankless at times. It can feel like a trial, as we read about in James. Who is someone who needs your love and care right now? This week, offer care to that person. Love them. Persevere in doing good for them. As Dustin said, be a light. This might mean caring for a family member, taking a meal to a neighbor, or even buying a cup of coffee for the homeless man you walk past on your way to work. In other words, extend grace to someone (a real test is to extend grace to someone who you think doesn't deserve it), and continue to do so even if it is difficult. Notice what happens as you persevere through the "trial" of putting yourself out for another person.

SESSION NOTES

(Hebrews 4:16, NIV)

Let us then approach God's throne of grace with confidence, so that we may receive mercy and find grace to help us in our time of need.

HOPE

WORTHY OF PURPOSE

[7]

Through this study, you have learned about what it means to have a relationship with God—not just to know about God, but to know him deeply. To truly trust him, even when you face challenging circumstances. You can put your faith and trust in God, because he is faithful, and he is trustworthy.

Because of this, we have hope. In the Bible, hope is not just a vague longing or wishing, but a confident expectation. Like a child trusts a loving parent, we trust God will care for us and meet our needs. We can know he's always eager to be with us. We are worthy of his attention and affection. That is what gives us hope, no matter our circumstances. And that hope can help us discover our purpose—our own transformational adventure.

In this final lesson, we're going to talk about what it means to be a son or daughter of God, and how that gives us hope—for this life and the life to come.

OPEN

◆ *What's one idea or concept from our last meeting that stuck with you?*

_____

_____

_____

//

◆ *Tell about a time when, despite difficult circumstances, you experienced hope.*

_____

_____

_____

WATCH VIDEO

WATCH THE VIDEO FOR THIS SESSION NOW.
VIDEO ACCESS: http://www.TransformationalAdventure.com/hope

SESSION NOTES

1. God speaks through _____ to bring _____ to others.

2. God sees us as _____ sons and daughters.

3. God promises us a _____ and a _____ .

_____

_____

_____

_____

_____

_____

READ

Hebrews 6:10-12, 17-20, NKJV

[10] For God is not unjust to forget your work and labor of love which you have shown toward His name, in that you have ministered to the saints, and do minister. [11] And we desire that each one of you show the same diligence to the full assurance of hope until the end, [12] that you do not become sluggish, but imitate those who through faith and patience inherit the promises.

[17] Thus God, determining to show more abundantly to the heirs of promise the immutability of His counsel, confirmed it by an oath, [18] that by two immutable things, in which it is impossible for God to lie, we might have strong consolation, who have fled for refuge to lay hold of the hope set before us.

[19] This hope we have as an anchor of the soul, both sure and steadfast, and which enters the Presence behind the veil, [20] where the forerunner has entered for us, even Jesus, having become High Priest forever according to the order of Melchizedek.

RESPOND

◆ In the video, Alan shared about a conversation he had with a stranger on a plane. He said, "God created us to be in relationship with each other. I began learning how to receive the love of God for someone else, how to flush myself, flush my mind to get out of the way for God to do his work." How can you set aside your own agenda to let God's love flow through you to others? How does "getting out of the way" build patience in us?

_____

_____

◆ Alan shared how God gave him a vision of a wonderful meal set before him, but said he didn't feel worthy enough to sit at the table with God, even though God invited him to be there. He realized that he was a child of God, and that he was worthy to sit at the table. "I didn't get how close God wanted to be with me," he said. What might keep someone from feeling worthy to sit at the table with God?

_____

_____

◆ How does knowing you are a child of God enable you to love other people?

_____

_____

◆ In Hebrews 6, we read about "the hope set before us." What is this hope? What does it give to us?

_____

_____

◆ What does the phrase "an anchor of the soul" mean to you? What promise is implied in this idea? Where do you find yourself drifting and in need of an anchor?

_____

_____

◆ When we embrace hope, we find our purpose. As you've experienced this study, what purpose has God has laid on your heart? What do you sense he's calling you to? Are you willing to take the adventure and go there? Whether it is moving to another city, taking another job, or even just getting into a row boat, God has an adventure for each of us. What next step is God prompting you to take on your own transformational adventure?

_____

_____

_____

DIVE DEEPER

(This section is for personal study between meetings.)

¹⁰ Finally, my brethren, be strong in the Lord and in the power of His might. ¹¹ Put on the whole armor of God, that you may be able to stand against the wiles of the devil. ¹² For we do not wrestle against flesh and blood, but against principalities, against powers, against the rulers of the darkness of this age, against spiritual hosts of wickedness in the heavenly places. ¹³ Therefore take up the whole armor of God, that you may be able to withstand in the evil day, and having done all, to stand.

Ephesians 6:10-13
NKJV

◆ *What sort of beings does verse 12 describe?*

_____

_____

◆ *Have you ever experienced challenges that feel like a spiritual battle? How did you respond?*

_____

_____

_____

◆ *What does this passage tell us will allow us to stand up against evil?*

_____

_____

_____

◆ *Optional further study: Look up this verse in your Bible or online, and read its context. What does the "whole armor of God" consist of?*

_____

_____

²⁰ I eagerly expect and hope that I will in no way be ashamed, but will have sufficient courage so that now as always Christ will be exalted in my body, whether by life or by death.
²¹ For to me, to live is Christ and to die is gain.

Philippians 1:20-21

NIV

◆ *Alan came to a place where he felt able to release his own life, to stop fearing death. And the hope and patience he'd longed for came when he was able to experience that "release of life." What do you think it means to release life? What gets in the way of your being able to release your life to God?*

_____

_____

_____

◆ *What does it mean to say "to live is Christ and to die is gain"? What would you do differently if you truly believed this? What is one change you can make to step toward this attitude?*

_____

_____

_____

²² We know that the whole creation has been groaning as in the pains of childbirth right up to the present time. ²³ Not only so, but we ourselves, who have the firstfruits of the Spirit, groan inwardly as we wait eagerly for our adoption to sonship, the redemption of our bodies. ²⁴ For in this hope we were saved. But hope that is seen is no hope at all. Who hopes for what they already have? ²⁵ But if we hope for what we do not yet have, we wait for it patiently. ²⁶ In the same way, the Spirit helps us in our weakness. We do not know what we ought to pray for, but the Spirit himself intercedes for us through wordless groans.

Romans 8:22–26

NIV

◆ *How does this passage describe the connection between hope and patience?*

_____

_____

◆ *What do you think it means to be adopted as a son or daughter of God? (See also Galatians 4:1-7.)*

_____

_____

◆ *In this passage, and in the video, heartfelt prayer is described as deep groaning. Have you ever prayed so fervently that you found yourself in a place of groaning? If so, how did this experience impact your relationship with God?*

_____

_____

GROANING
Romans 8:23, 26

The Bible refers several times to groaning prayer—a deep, intense prayer. Jesus prayed for Lazarus (John 11:33) this way before raising him from the dead. The Bible also says that the Holy Spirit prays for us in this way. Groaning prayers go far beyond simply reciting words, and they're not eve heartfelt praise and worship. They come from our pain and difficulty, from a place deeper than words, presenting as a deep sighing that expresses travail. These groaning prayers also indicate th we are aligned with God, in a way that words cannot fully express.

While we may not want to be in those painful places, they allow us to express our deepest longing to God. And what a comfort that the Holy Spirit prays for us with similar intensity and depth. Whe we don't know what to pray, the Spirit prays for us. God feels our pain and comforts us even wher we can't find the words to pray.

RESOURCES

POWERS AND PRINCIPALITIES
Ephesians 6:12

The things we can see, taste, and touch—the natural world—is not all there is. There is also a supernatural world that influences our experience. When we feel God's love or presence, or even have a vision as Alan did (where God invited him to be with Him at the table), we get a glimpse of the supernatural. This supernatural world contains forces of both good and evil. We battle against unseen, supernatural forces of evil, identified as "powers and principalities." We need to be aware, but we do not need to be afraid. God is our protector. His "whole armor" is available to us. His power will enable us to have victory.

ACTION STEPS

Now that you've completed this study, what do you think your next step in your relationship with God should be? What particular situation is he asking you to trust him with?

In the video, Alan said that God told him to "be the spark that ignites and unites a nation under God." What do you think it means to be a spark? In what way do you want to be a spark? What purpose do you sense God preparing you for?

SESSION NOTES

APPENDIX

Here are the completed "revelations" from each video:

Session 1: Salvation: The Wake-Up Call of a Lifetime
1. Acting religious does not make you a Christian.
2. Thinking is not believing.
3. Feeling comfortable often means we're deceived.

Session 2: Brokenness: A Death Sentence That Brought Life
1. God can be trusted.
2. God's love gives us hope and peace.
3. God loves us through other people.

Session 3: Restoration: Pain That Brought Healing
1. Facing trials we can choose to rest.
2. Resting in God builds our trust in him.
3. Trusting in God brings hope and restoration.

Session 4: Power: An Anchor in the Storm
1. Pray continuously and confidently.
2. Speak boldly and positively.
3. Clarify your priorities.

Session 5:   Forgiveness: Love That Changes Everything

1.   God's love is unconditional.
2.   God's love transforms our character and identity.
3.   God's love enables us to forgive.

Session 6:   Grace: The Power to Turn It All Around

1.   Brokenness readies us for change.
2.   Surrender brings eternal perspective.
3.   Receiving God's love allows us to love others.

Session 7:   Hope: Worthy of Purpose

1.   God speaks through us to bring hope to others.
2.   God sees us as worthy sons and daughters.
3.   God promises us a hope and a purpose.

BOOKS (AVAILABLE ON AMAZON)

THE HEART OF IT ALL

At 37 years of age, I thought I had the best of what life had to offer. But after years of pushing myself to win at all costs, I got the wake-up call of a lifetime. I was used to being the leader: the guy with the football scholarship, the rising young professional, the head of a beautiful family. I had it all...or so I thought... After months of chest pain, I found myself lying on a table in the doctor's office. I heard my nurse cuss underneath his breath. He was staring at an angiogram of my heart and it looked deadly. Between the stress tests and the angiogram, my cardiologist revealed that I had two 90 degree bends in my Left Anterior Descending Artery. It was 98% blocked, and most other patients in my condition wouldn't be alive. Within five years, I had two heart surgeries...one physical and one spiritual. I am a miracle. What He's done has blown me away...and it's available for all of us.

HIDDEN BLESSINGS FROM CANCER

"I have shaken hands with the grips of death...not once, not twice, but three times...all on varying occasions. I have had a doctor look me square in the eye and somberly say, 'You should've died. We do not know how you're still alive.' Several years later, it appeared that my cancer had metastasized and I had a very small chance of survival. And yet, after this, I find myself in continual healing and restoration from head to toe - body, soul and spirit. I want to share with you what changed my life." - Alan Williams

HIDDEN BLESSINGS FROM CHEMO

"YOU WILL SPEND 1 YEAR IN BED." When the doctor told me about chemotherapy and its effects, I learned how to rest and trust, hearing God's voice louder than my circumstance or the voice of man. Some say that faith requires you to get out of the boat - but for me, faith looked like getting out of bed and getting into a boat. When the doctor told me that I would be in bed for a year, my wife and I decided to develop a bucket list. These goals gave me hope. I started sculling - and with the dosage of chemotherapy that I was receiving - I shouldn't have been able to do it...But I did. I want to share with you how I made it through the worst part of chemo treatments and how I went from being fearful to thankful in daily living.

THE POWER OF A CAREGIVER

"When I heard Alan say 'I have cancer,' a wave of fear rolled over me. It sent my insides spinning. After the initial shock of hearing about Alan's diagnosis of cancer, I knew everything was about to change. We had lived self-sufficient lives. We could do it all on our own. But this was bigger than we were. We couldn't work our way out of this one. We knew we were going to need some help.

Even though it was difficult, I found strength, learned how to master the waves of change, and provided support and care to my husband...It changed everything for our family, our marriage, and even Alan's health. I want to share with you what influenced and anchored me during one of the most challenging times of our lives." - Inda Williams